WHEN THE ENEMY
Enters In

JACQUELINE KING

ACKNOWLEDGEMENTS

Thank God, for without problems
there are no provisions.

I thank my daughters who
loved no matter what.

Thanks to my friend, Priscilla,
who never interfered
with my life.

Special thanks to Melita Freeman,
for both her editing and
publishing guidance.

To the men and women who
are enduring what I suffered.
May you be encouraged, enlightened,
and empowered throughout
your trial for deliverance.

CONTENTS

PROLOGUE

Imagine walking up to your perfect dream home. A home that took years to establish and build. You strut closer with a sense of security, knowing that inside the door lies a welcoming warmth and an adoring love of family.

When you step onto the porch, you see the lock has been tampered with. Chips of golden paint and jagged pieces of wood lay scattered around your feet.

You sense there was a break in, a forced entry. Someone crept in and caused much damage.

Cautiously approaching each large room of your open floor plan, you notice new items missing…a digital stereo…a fancy flat screen television…Gone are your valuable possessions.

These may be what the thief desperately desires to steal behind your locked doors. In my case, it was my marriage.

Keep your heart with all diligence,
for out of it springs the issues of life.
(Proverbs 4:2)

Chapter One

A ROUGH BEGINNING

It was the summer of 1992, May to be exact. I was twenty-six years old. I knew of God, but was not serving Him at the time.

My brother invited his family and friends to a birthday party. He had previously installed two large speakers in my cherry-red Ford Probe. The sound was premium.

Remember to thank him again, I mentally noted, while driving through the projects to the event.

It was around 8:00 p.m. when I arrived. I sat with everyone and mingled while enjoying the vibe of the atmosphere. In between conversations, I stepped outside to check on my beaming vehicle.

My third time around, a young man stopped me. He was dark-skinned and very fine; his carved physique bulking through a fitted black shirt adding to the sex appeal.

"What is your name?" He asked boldly.

"Tina," I answered and was flattered by the attention he gave.

"I'm Greg." His rich baritone pitch elevated over the boom of the music.

He walked along with me and joined my circle. When the party was over, we lingered. Then he asked if I would drive him to the store. We left the store and sat in front of his house awhile.

He shared that recently having been discharged from prison, he had served four of a sixteen year sentence.

"God cut the time, because He has a work for me to do."

This did not register with me though, because I was too mesmerized by his heart-shaped lips, plus I sensed no fear at the time.

As we further opened up about our lives and future, he decided to invite me in...to the living room...to the bedroom. There we sat on the edge of a neatly tucked bed sharing deeply about ourselves.

The next thing I knew, we were passionately making love until 6 o'clock the next morning.

I left his house and he called me the next day--or should I say the same day, asking me to come over again.

From that moment to when the trouble began, we were nearly inseparable.

My boyfriend was out of town. One evening before picking up the phone to answer his call, I heard a voice.

"Greg is your husband."

At this time, I was in a traditional Baptist church and we never talked about the voice of God.

I turned skeptically, looking for anyone around, but saw no one. Again, the phone rang, and so did the voice repeat itself.

"Greg is your husband."

Looking up I said, "Oh, no, he's not. He's

just a booty call. I was married to a buck wild man before, and I am NOT marrying this man. He is too much for me!"

"He is your husband," still the voice insisted.

Within days, while riding around in the car, Greg asked what I was doing later.

"I have plans for the evening," I answered, expecting to reunite later with my beau.

"You're not going anywhere, you're my woman now," he pronounced.

I smiled at this. *He knows what he wants. I like that.*

He seemed different from my boyfriend who kept making light of his commitment. Greg communicated his intentions more readily and was three years older than I. This guy also seemed more mature than my boyfriend. So, from that day on, I invested more time into this relationship.

Four months flew by. Greg and I were sitting outside a night club. I swooned with romantic energy. "In October, we're getting married on Halloween."

He laughed and with biting humor replied, "The trick will be on you, because

I'm not showing up."

I joined in with laughter to cover my deflated feelings.

"By the way, I have never seen your two girls," he added.

"Well, I'm dating and don't bring men around my kids until I know for sure we have a good relationship. You have to understand, I'm raising girls and I have to teach and show them better things so they can respect me."

When October rolled around, I finally introduced Greg to my babies. Necie, who was eight years old, drew back a little. Christine was seven and instantly attached to him.

He agreed we should get married six months later. So, we drove out a few miles to Marshall County, Kentucky, to get the license, then over to a preacher's house to share the great news.

"We want to get married!" We exclaimed, in my blue jean shorts and his khaki tan pants.

"Do you have a witness?" The preacher asked.

"I will be their witness," offered his

wife. So, the pastor married us.

My heart was elated at the sight of my handsome, new husband.

During our first year, everything seemed perfect; but the day I said "I do," I never imagined that bars of imprisonment were in store.

We lived in the projects. Having ups and downs didn't derail us to separate. The vow states "for better or for worse," right?

Management raised our apartment rent to $300 a month, so we had to move in with my mother.

I was unemployed. During this period, my husband usually earned $95 weekly. He did eventually find a better job. So, we moved into an apartment.

I started working also, and we moved again: to a house on Beard Street...from there to Donna Street...to Goodlett Circle...then to 1011 Birkshire Drive. We were moving on up!

With every move we advanced, but the final move was where I discovered the trouble. Approaching our third year of marriage, while still on Donna Street, Greg began to stay away from home. Whenever he would visit his family, he left me.

"I'm going with you to see Mama Dupree," I insisted on visiting my mother-in-law.

"You're not family," he uttered selfishly. Then I arranged sleepovers for my children at my mother's, thinking he would take me out, because we were kid-free. "Tina, I am planning to stay home this weekend." Now, he only came home when the kids were away, which was not often.

My husband started accusing me of cheating. He became cruel and violent.

We argued and fought every weekend, and the fights became increasingly dreadful the more we engaged in them.

One afternoon, my cousin invited me to dinner. A friend of Greg's and mine was there. He was thrilled about his new business opening soon. I offered to come by and see it one day. He replied, "Why not now?" So, he drove me to the building.

As we rode, Greg called me asking me to come home. I informed him that I was nowhere near home.

Our friend drove me back to dinner, and I drove home.

Greg was patient in waiting on me. His interrogation was thorough, as he claimed to have found out I was with Roman. I asked why the mistrust and doubt, since this man had always been a mutual friend.

He snatched my hair and dragged me down the hallway; and from the hallway to the kitchen, holding my hair in his fist for about an hour and a half. Hearing my hair strands tearing from the root, the pain was so intense I prayed hard. Every now and then I screamed, "Please, Lord, tell him to let go."

One particular Sunday he was frustrated. It was storming and thundering outside. As with the heavy rains beating against our window panes, he furiously interrupted my rest.

I know you're cheating!"

"Don't come home with that mess. I have to work!" I interrupted sharply.

Greg was so angry that he threw me on the floor and penned me down with his knees pressed against my arms. My limbs were numb and pierced with pain. When he picked himself up from off me, I ran outside a mile to get away. I wanted never to return and cried for the brutality, but went there anyway to dress myself for work.

Going through nights of horror at home, then to a professional setting in the day was like walking through a revolving door.

Greg was also very demanding and controlling. It was his way or no way at all.

His father, Daddy Dupree, was said to have a reputation for keeping women in the house. I heard stories by their family, how Mr. Dupree used to have their mom stay in a room all day until he returned.

Greg began behaving similarly. He hated for me to sit on the porch when he was away. Whenever married couples lived beside us, their husbands sat on the porch after mine arrived. Of course, it was because he thought the men were trying to talk to me.

He couldn't watch me and be away from home too, so he demanded before leaving, "Don't go outside!" I parted the draperies several times and saw him cruising around the house to see if I obeyed.

My child, Necie realized what he was doing. Once, when he closed the door she opened it and said, "Mommy, if you want to go out the door, go!" She pointed her tiny finger outside.

Out of the mouths of babes! I glanced into her innocent eyes then replied, "Some things you will know by and by, a mother does for the sake of peace."

I was a homebody; so, my husband's absence and control issues did not occur to me at the onset. Not until he left increasingly and became violent did I begin to internalize neglect and loneliness while raising my children.

Nearly ready to file for divorce, I held onto a flicker of hope.

Greg and I shared similar spiritual beliefs and culture. We both knew about Christ, but neither of us had a personal relationship with Him.

We both knew the church scene, having been attending all our lives, but had not truly offered ourselves.

And we both grew up in the projects, but our dreams were bigger than our small worlds.

After we married, I began attending his church which provided more faith based teaching.

One day he came to the house and said, "I believe I'm a minister. I've always dreamed of being a minister, ever since a little boy." I didn't say a word. I just listened.

Later that night, I had a strange dream. *My husband repeatedly came home from a night club. The first night he urinated in our linen closet.*

The second night he moved the sheets off the shelf, and climbed on it to go to sleep. A woman came up to me and told me my husband was under the curse of witches. So, I grabbed my kids and went to get his mother for help. My mother-in-law came over and got him out of the closet and tucked him in bed.

On the third night he arrived home and shared with me how God spoke to him in the club, while he was trying to get high smoking weed.

At the end, he did become a minister.

So, when he mentioned again that he wanted to be a minister, I said, "Okay, maybe you are a minister."

That Sunday morning as I prepared to attend worship service, Greg ranted and raved about me being attracted to someone there; to which I replied was ridiculous.

Eventually, he crept over into the other

room, then turned on a gospel radio station. Someone from Tennessee by the name of Bishop Patterson was preaching a sermon. On my way out, my husband was ready to tag along.

We had a guest speaker on that same day. Evangelist Dixon called me forward and prayed for me, saying there was a ministry in me.

After she finished speaking, she gave an alter call.

A church member kindly ushered Greg forward.

The evangelist asked if he wanted to be saved. He answered, "No."

She replied, "Yes, you do. It's time for you to stop running from your calling."

God saved both of us at the same time.

But I see another law in my members warring against the law of my mind and bringing me into captivity to the law of sin which is in my members.
(Romans 7:23)

Chapter Two

THE TURN AROUND

God worked a complete 360-degree change in Greg's life. He came home and trashed his beer and cigarettes. Where he was so hateful, controlling, and full of pride, God humbled him down and he was definitely a new person.

Every Sunday we attended church. Each revival we sat closer to the front just to listen and learn.

We grew together, discovering our gifts in business and finance. God gave us wisdom for entrepreneurship. We owned two facilities. A restaurant and a bowling alley next door to it.

We tithed on every penny we earned, and God was doing His thing!

Meanwhile, our pastor noticed giftings in us to inspire others, and encouraged us to testify of the Lord's goodness. My husband spoke with charisma. Everything this man did was breathtaking!

And God continued to bless us. The more He blessed us, the more I could see changes for the good in Gregory.

My husband knew that I always kept the house clean. When I could not because of illness, he would stay with me the first day and hire a sitter to help with the other days.

He instructed, "More than anything, make sure my wife is comfortable."

Every car we had previously owned, he alone selected. Now, my opinions were important to him.

One time I answered, "We have two growing kids. Let's get a van." He bought it.

Another time I suggested, "We should get a recreational vehicle to take on family vacations." He purchased a wide travel trailer with extra amenities.

The man spoiled me. ANYTHING--and I do mean anything I asked for, he got it.

He washed my car and kept gas in it.

Sometimes, he came home and gave me extra money just to go shopping.

Whenever I needed a break away from the house, he put me up in a hotel room for a day.

He brought home "just because" gifts-- expensive gifts.

Once, I cried for having to change a light bulb, because I never had to when he was around.

These kinds of treatments went on for five years and I did not have a problem with it.

We were inseparable. We shopped for groceries together and people began to recognize us. When they saw me without him, they asked, "Where is your husband?"

"On the other aisle," was my usual response.

"I knew he was not far from you," they would admire.

He took me with him everywhere. When he went to play basketball, he had me by his side.

When he left the house without me, he called on his way home and always came in before sundown.

I spent two weeks in Tennessee with my sister, after receiving a phone call from her that she had double pneumonia. I cried for having to leave.

Gregory and I talked on the phone all day and night until falling asleep. When the two weeks were over, he picked me up. Boy, I was happy to see him!

"I want a son," he expressed one day. He was loving to my girls, and I knew he would make an exceptional dad to our son. So, we eagerly set ourselves for a new addition to our family.

A friend complimented me that she wished her family was as close as mine.

I remember saying, "Girl, I went through to get here, but God!"

Now that Gregory was home more often, he studied the Bible all the time. My husband became increasingly skillful in the Word.

When I rehashed an issue, he looked at me until I finished fussing.

"Dinner is ready," he said.

"What are you going to say?" I urged.

"It takes two to argue."

I'd smile and walk away.

Staying focused on creating a loving atmosphere, keeping the kids in order, and maintaining a spotless home, were among my efforts of insuring a blessed family life.

I was learning to pray through my house and anoint it.

If an argument brewed up between the girls, I made sure it was resolved before their father came home from work.

When he arrived, all he had to do was eat dinner and rest. I kept dinner on the table, unless we ate out.

I helped pay the bills and cut the yard to lighten the load.

God was so good to us. Life was good. We were good.

Refusing to break God's Word, Gregory's faith was truly revealed to me in 1996. The news alerted that we should take necessary precautions for a water shortage.

I saved water so I could wash clothes and prepare for it.

My husband did not budge. He assured, "God will make a way." When the media said there would be no gas in the service stations, it seemed almost everyone in the city filled their tanks. Yet, he insisted, "God will make a way."

Gregory had such peace in his relationship with God that nothing moved him.

I was in awe of the peace that surrounded my husband, even in the midst of trouble. I said to God, "The God that my husband is serving, let me serve that same God!"

God was our main subject in the morning and in the evening, at the dinner table and at night.

Obeying His Word and living under its construction made my husband a far better man than when he had been staying away from family and home.

We were extremely happy and our lives were greater during these five years by surrendering to God.

Delight thyself also in the Lord;
and he shall give thee the desires of thine heart.
(Psalms 37:4)

24

Chapter Three

THE VISION

My husband was so wonderful to me, I never would have imagined it would be a set up for an even worse nightmare.

Cooking his choice meal of the day, calling him on my lunch break, and visiting Mama Dupree, all turned around to the advantage of a calculating husband. Those faithful duties came back to haunt me: My good deeds seemed in vain.

My performance did become predictable

and summed up to be one total objective for him, "I know where my wife is." Insecurity, you think?

Fast approaching our sixth spiritual birthday, our pastor acknowledged the call of God on my husband. So, Gregory became a minister in training.

At first, we did not feel appropriately dressed among fellowshipping believers. So, I bought him fine suits to wear.

He was donned so nicely, my mother-in-law said, "Tone that boy down. You got him too clean in the pulpit."

"Mommy, that's my husband and he's out front. He's supposed to look good," I defended.

Still assuming things were perfect, I decided to ask my husband for a bigger house.

"Go look for one," he answered agreeably.

I found a lovely home and went to visit a realtor to get things set up. We bought it. But, something happened when we moved in to our new place.

Eventually, my husband started to get the big head, and was no longer interested in doing all those wonderful things for me.

He ceased to come home before sunset.

He stopped calling me when he was on his way home from playing ball.

Also, he wanted another car. It was my understanding that it was to get us to and from church. So, we went to a Cadillac dealer to look. He viewed the first few automobiles contemptuously. We searched further. This time it was a large, Chevrolet Avalanche he rejected. Then he spotted a black, Chevrolet Camaro.

I thought it was odd to purchase a sports car seated for two, because we were a family of four. When I touched the car, a vision immediately appeared before me. I saw young women surrounding my husband, while he behaved immaturely. Moreover, I felt him cheating with them.

"No, Gregory, not this car," I instantly reacted.

We bought the car anyway. Was I content with the purchase? No, but curious as to why my opinion no longer mattered.

Later that night, God shared again with me a vision. Gregory left me for another woman. Then, I saw a long, dark line and a view of myself at the altar working in ministry with a man. God did not reveal who the man was. I woke up from my slumber feeling perplexed. It felt so real.

"Gregory! Gregory, are you cheating on me?" I asked one morning during twilight hours.

"Woman, lie down with that foolishness. Ain't nobody doing anything!" He was convincing.

"Okay," I conceded and went back to sleep.

As months crept on, seeing my husband change was disheartening. He didn't quite have that glow on him.

The man of whom God had worked a 360-degree transformation on, was steadily falling backward.

Arguments fueled more regularly. He was, as once the person before, controlling and demanding.

Also, his music started to transition from clean to profanity at our bowling alley.

This produced a lower class of younger people, especially females, who dressed provocatively.

He had previously ministered to some

young men, but now they replaced his peers in basketball and all other activities.

I did not have a problem with him spending time with the youth, but my spirit did not have peace about it.

Also, our establishment had a large pool table. He began spending most of his time in that area.

One Friday night, my daughters were at the bowling alley with their father. They were calling friends on his cellular phone. He received a message from a lady which read, "What are you doing?"

"Where are you?" My daughters texted back.

"It's none of your business," the lady replied.

About a week passed, and my daughters said they could no longer withhold what they discovered.

"Mom, Dad has a lady friend who's texting him."

I inquired more on the matter and they explained. Necie borrowed his phone. She called the woman who had texted several indiscreet message to her dad.

The mysterious female began to argue

with my daughter.

I called my husband and asked him what was going on.

He came home and told us that the woman had booked a surprise party. He further stated how rude our girls were.

So, I asked Gregory for his phone to investigate, but he yanked it back.

Since I started studying God's Word, His voice was more recognizable. I walked to my bedroom asking Him what was going on; stating quietly, *Whatever it is, You will reveal it to me.*

The entire situation provoked mixed feelings. I did not want to go against what my girls said, but I couldn't go against my husband's explanation either.

Shortly afterward, his footsteps followed mine. When he walked in, he looked at me for a long time and spoke. "I'm not doing what you think I'm doing."

I hoped nothing was going on, but feared the obvious.

He walked into the kids' room and said, "You thought that was going to hurt your mother, but she's not hurt."

After this incident, my husband started

to go out every day from 7:00 p.m. to 1:00 a.m. I endured months of this and was becoming fed up.

"Things have gone too far. You are going to go out of that door and meet something you're not able to let go."

"Is that right?" He grinned before walking out.

"You are no match for the enemy," I replied under my breath.

The truth unfolded after months. We were arguing so much that I kept seeking God for answers. Then I decided to call our pastor to tell him about Greg's behavior.

"Do you think Greg would call me?" He inquired.

At the rate my husband was going, I knew that calling the pastor was not on his agenda.

My voice uttered in despair, "No, Sir."

He asked me where Greg spent most of his time, and I informed at him the bowling alley.

"As God leads me, I will approach him."

He sounded careful in answering, and encouraged me to get on my knees to seek God. I did what he said, but yet heard little.

Days later, I called back. "I still don't

know, pastor."

He told me to open my heart and God will reveal. I prayed, but every time God was ready to show me, my heart fluttered.

Even though there was a lot going on, the more I prayed to God, the closer I felt to Him. So close that I could literally smell His freshness.

Then, one night I opened up and asked the Lord to condition my heart to accept what He really wanted to show me.

He did. I saw faces of other women. It was piercing. I lost it!

When Greg arrived home that day, I said nothing to him. In the middle of the night, I saw that he had an extra phone.

Tiptoeing around the side of his bed to grab it, I scrolled through his text messages. While in the restroom, I saw there were calls by the same number.

"Call me," they stated. I wrote the number down and quickly placed the phone back where he left it.

The next morning I asked, "Are you going to tell me you're cheating and who the lady is?"

I'm not doing anything. You're the one

cheating!"

"This day I will close this chapter of the book. Before the sun goes down, God will reveal who she is!"

Gregory left the house to go to work.

I had the number and didn't know what to do with it. My sister-in-law whose occupation is at a phone company, gave me a name to match the number from the phone. She provided me with a home and work address, the whole package.

The next morning, I traveled twenty miles away to the suburban town of Trigg County. That home was vacant. So, I visited the next address on the list.

On the way, I called Greg and asked cleverly, "Where do you get your tire shine products from?

"The town's auto shop," he answered hesitantly.

"Okay, I'm going there today to get some.
"Oh--no--no, I will get it when I get off."
"That's okay, I'm almost there."

He quickly hung up the phone, barely letting me finish.

When I walked in the store, I did not know what the mystery woman looked like, but when inquiring at the service desk, I discovered she was the manager. So, I made my presence known.

When my husband came home, we started arguing about where I had been. He turned to leave, but first whirled around spurting hurtful words.

I blurted out, "Her name is Stephanie Green, she lives in Trigg County, and her phone number is 270-333-3333!"

He stood in shock, as if I had just revealed his darkest secret.

"I told you before the sun went down that God would reveal it to me," I boasted.

It was evening. Greg left and stayed gone even longer than usual, two weeks. I did not know where he was, nor did I bother to look.

When he came back, he bluntly informed me that he would be moving in with her that night.

"I'm leaving for good. I'm not happy, and I want out of the marriage."

I decided to get a hotel room to more privately seek God's face.

That same night my husband called me constantly, but I did not answer the phone.

Hours later, he called again asking where

I was.

"Why?"

"Because, I can't leave you, I need to talk to you."

So, I told him that I was in a hotel and he met me there. We talked and he shared that he told Stephanie he was leaving me, but the Lord told him to go back to his wife. The following day we drove home.

When we pulled into the garage, the words *I'm not happy*, played over and over again in my mind.

How could he not be happy with our marriage? I mean, everything was fine until the enemy decided to creep in.

I looked at him with a heavy heart and communicated how I felt. "That hurt me. I don't know if I can ever hear you say that you're not happy."

"Tina, I know what I got, but I didn't know what I was getting. I hope I will never hurt you like that again."

Again, the words rehearsed in my mind. *I hope… I hope I will never hurt you again.*

His sincerity was now in question. *Could this mean he may leave me again for someone else? Am I subject to be in this same situation again, left to feeling rejected and abandoned on a whim?*

I walked into the living room and God spoke, "He has a problem. Tell him that if he wants to change, My Word says that he can. If he stays out there, the next girl will be finer and younger, and it will be harder for him to come back home. That very thing will destroy him." I did as God instructed.

Four months did my husband display an earnest desire to reconcile.

He was more considerate to call when he was out.

He came in at more appropriate hours in the evening.

I assumed he was on the road to recovery, but could not help but notice that both his conversation and dress apparel continued to regress.

His words used to be Godly, but had now reverted to street talk.

His pants, which used to be dressy, were now baggy.

My mother-in-law who was a Godly woman, sensed Greg was into something destructive and came to visit. When she arrived, he briefly greeted her and left. This was another unusual act of behavior, being that we always enjoyed keeping company with her.

"Tina, God told me to come over here yesterday, but I didn't. This is your test and you can win. Don't let no devil take your marriage," she exhorted.

For the word of God is living and powerful
and sharper than any twoedged sword,
piercing even to the dividing of soul and spirit,
and of joints and marrow
and is a discerner of the thoughts
and intents of the heart.
(Hebrews 4:12)

Chapter Four

STEPHANIE'S WEB

What do you want to do for your birthday, mom?" My daughters were thoughtful to ask.

"I never had a birthday party," I replied.

They gave me my first party and my husband celebrated with us.

He gave me a card with forty dollars in it. Then he led me in a dance. I had not danced in nine years, since he and I had first dated. As we slid across the floor, I heard, "Greg is used to this." *I know he's seeing another woman, but clubbing again?*

I startled back and inquired. "Greg, God said you are used to this."

"What *this*?"

"This dancing, drinking and clubbing."

"Woman, stop being silly. God didn't tell you that."

Two weeks after, Christine came up to me.

"Momma, I'm going to show you a picture of this girl on Facebook who parties with her mom."

When she brought me the picture, I looked at it and said, "Wow, that's sad for a mother and daughter to be out partying like that." Looking closer at the picture on the social media website, I realized it was Greg in the background, holding a drink in his hand.

Immediately approaching him for a confession, I exclaimed, "Greg, this is you!"

"That's not me."

"You think I don't know my own husband?" I told him that nobody held his hand around a glass with fingers balled up in

39

the manner he did; and besides that, the ring he wore on his finger was the same one as in the picture.

He still denied it. So, I went into his closet and pulled out each piece of clothing that matched his outfit in the picture, even down to the shoes. Then, he walked away.

Now, I stood thinking, *I am not only dealing with a liar and a cheater, but much more.* I exploded. "You're lying, cheating, drinking, clubbing, manipulating, not taking care of home, and accusing me every time I turn around!"

"Get up, I need you to see something," God's voice spoke at 2 a.m. So, I put on clothes and started driving. Passing by an apartment complex, I heard, "Greg is there." *I don't see his car,* I thought drowsily, while turning back to head home. "Look to your left."

There it was. His car was parked in front of her house.

"I am sick," I texted him instinctively. "Come home."

Then I grabbed one of my exercise dumbbells from off the back floorboard, and mad dashed forward.

When he walked out of the door, I let him have it with a three pounder in my hand! The enemy has his way of getting people out of character.

"I just got here," he voiced repeatingly. "I'm not doing anything."

"No, you're not doing anything tonight but getting this whooping!" I continued pounding.

We arrived home, continuing to fight and argue. I had lost control, but ran into my room and grabbed my Bible. The presence of the Lord was heavy on me. I turned to Deuteronomy 28, and quoted loudly the results of disobedience.

Once I started reading, Greg spun around several times as if he was on a merry-go-round, then ran outside.

He attempted to distract me in a peculiar manner. "Look at that cat, Tina! Look at that cat!"

I kept reading and he ran back inside the house.

After scrambling through my closet for a book called "Clean House, Strong House," I told him that I would call out every demonic name until I hit the one in him.

Greg ran to the bedroom and shut the door. He locked it and turned the television on loudly. "Don't call out anything you can't handle," He yelled. "You don't know what you're doing!"

The next morning he had to preach, believe it or not. I went with him to the eleven o'clock service, though he didn't want me to.

The entire time I sat there staring, but he couldn't look at me. As I watched him in the pulpit, I realized all the God in Greg was leaving.

When we returned home from church, we sat down and talked. I confronted him about Stephanie.

Greg finally spoke up. He seemed distant and spoke quietly. "Tina, I'm not happy."

I stared at him and asked him to repeat what he had just said, because in my heart, I wanted to hear differently.

"I'm not happy, I've desired to tell you for a while."

The words that he so easily found to verbalize were tearing me apart. I grew speechless as tears streamed down my face.

He finally revealed, "I have been seeing Stephanie over a period of nine years. I met her at a car show early on. She tried to sell me some tire shine, and it all started like that. I ended it once before, but she came back to me for prayer one day and things spiraled out of control.

I was stupefied. My mind went back to the total nine years of our marriage. How is it possible he has been seeing her all this time without my knowledge? *So, she was the cause from the very start?*

"You ministered to her alone? Why would you do that! You know the pastor told us to never privately counsel anyone."

I wanted to run. I wanted to stay. I wanted to cry. I wanted to fight. I stood up to do something--ANYTHING.

Being both overwhelmed and mentally senseless, I panicked. In a state of confusion, I left Gregory in the bedroom and headed toward the garage.

The crush had left me hopelessly sitting in a warm van, entrapped by garage doors and paneled walls. I switched on the ignition to run the heat full blast. *Why? me?* I pondered, while deliberately reclining the head rest back.

Hours later, he found me. While opening the sliding door of the vehicle, Greg shouted, "What are you doing? Are you trying to kill yourself?"

I guess--well--yes, I am, I thought; but was unable to speak by the inhaled toxic fumes.

He pulled me out of the car and walked me into the house, then left.

My next reaction was to get Stephanie. I wanted to beat her down! Isn't it funny how our initial response is to get the woman, not the man?

Yet, I found resolve. *So, what good would it do when they both know right from wrong? Greg is with who he wants to be with.*

Quickly accepting God's forgiveness for trying to kill myself, I moved on in His strength.

Stephanie's car got scratched up, and she told my husband I was the culprit.

"What are you talking about, I was home with you," I denied.

Greg agreed with her on the telephone. I was so hurt to know he was betraying me for his mistress, I exclaimed into his phone handle, "Baby, if he is doing this to his wife, what do you think he's going to do to you!" Then, I hung up on her and warned him, "Ya'll need to be careful, you are coming against a woman of God."

Stephanie came by my house soon afterward. She parked in front, while I emptied the trash out back. I came around and she drove off.

I called Greg, "Your woman just left my house. Keep your street women in the street."

He promptly contacted Stephanie by 3-way and asked if she stopped by. "Stop lying, Tina," he manipulated the conversation, "No one came by *your* house."

I sighed at this, "I'm not going to argue with you. I'm standing outside and I know what I saw."

He continued, "I don't sleep with you. I don't even touch you. We sleep in separate bedrooms."

"That came out of nowhere," I said, embarrassed that he exposed our private life to her.

When I saw Greg later, I gave him a few words I had been longing to say. "The next time you have her on the phone while you're talking to me! You're always taking up for her and you're doing it in my face.

Your day is coming. All hell is going to break loose on you. You are one disrespectful man and you call yourself a man of God."

Still clinging to faith for the man I once adored, I was not quite willing to relent to the devil or surrender my husband into the arms of another woman. I asked my husband if he would leave her, but he indicated no. His attitude was, *You can either deal with it or leave.* So, I dealt with it.

Meanwhile, God dealt with my heart to earnestly forgive the offenses of Stephanie. Yes, Stephanie--the other woman.

I told my husband that if I ever saw her, I was going to beat her down.

He replied, "You stay in a Godly woman's place."

A week later, I met her at the store. I said, "Stephanie, I need to talk to you."

Before I could say anything, God reminded me, "Forgive her."

She came over to where I was. I said, "As much as I want to get down with you, God will not let me. So, I'm here to say, I forgive you and my husband."

"What are you talking about?" She denied scornfully. It took everything in me not to go off on her. I said, "Stephanie, I know you are messing with my husband."

"Keep me out of y'all marriage. I don't have nothing to do with what you and your husband's got going on," she remarked.

"Stephanie, now--now, Stephanie. Please, I'm forgiving you. Just go on and walk away. Please, walk away." I was boiling.

The next day, I came home from work and entered into the bedroom. I saw Greg's closet door open and all his clothes were gone. I fell to my knees and asked God to help me bear this. Lying on the floor all night, I cried without sleep.

The next morning, I found scriptures and started praying in my closet. Every day that week I went into my closet, prayed and quoted scriptures on my marriage.

One day, when I left my closet, God said, "Go back and pray."

I said, "I am praying, Lord."

He said, "No, you are not praying my will."

I said with everything in me, "Forgive

me, God. Whether or not my husband comes back home, I choose to serve you."

God said, "Because of your confession to serve me, I will bring Greg back home."

About two days later, Greg came home and we sat in the garage talking about what he had done. We began to hug and cry together.

Stephanie opened a store which she named, Stephanie's Web.

God revealed to me about the word "web." He said that after a male spider mates with a certain female spider, the male spider dies. God said when my husband lay with Stephanie, he died spiritually.

Also, God showed me about Saul in the Bible. He told him not to "mingle with foreign women, because they will turn your heart."

I said, "God, what are foreign women?"

He said, "Any woman outside of your marriage."

True enough, the more my husband dabbled with her spirits, the more and stronger they attached onto him. I could see the darkness in his face.

Although, I did not know what God was fully telling me, I understood I had been in 'Stephanie's web" for nine years.

She liked to pull my strings by calling our home and parking in front of our yard. She showed no regard for me as Greg's wife, and he permitted her to treat me this way.

Soon, my husband started entering our home with unfamiliar scents on him.

He seemed completely oblivious to what was happening.

His going and coming was so disturbing that I was wearied, needing a place to rest.

We argued and fussed, but I was getting nowhere trying to get him to see.

One day, as he was coming in, I was going out with a packed garment bag. I told him I needed to get away for a few days.

When I returned, Greg had changed the locks and moved Stephanie into our home. So, I arranged an agreement with another local apartment manager for a temporary stay and paid a month's rent to stay there.

During this time, I circled around my street block each morning and saw Stephanie's car in our driveway.

I asked daily if she was living there, and

49

Greg replied, "No." I then asked God to move her out, because I was tired.

Soon after, Gregory called me and asked me if I wanted to move back. I answered readily.

He said he was moving her out, and when I come back, he didn't want me to make a sound. Just live in the back room and don't come out. I couldn't even cook unless it was for both of us. I do not know what he explained to her, but he manipulated the situation well, because I moved back in that Friday.

Stephanie saw Necie at a convenient store and boldly introduced herself.

My daughter called me; she was so upset. I left the house walking through the neighborhood, to go find that woman. Locating her at the community park, I warned her emphatically to never speak to my children again. "Don't even waive a hand at them. What you and Greg do, that's y'all. You can do it on the rooftop--I don't care, but don't ever say anything to my kids again!" I repeated.

Directly after that, a lady at the park approached me as I sat on a picnic table.

She overheard my conversation and began sharing her similar issue. Out of my pain, I began ministering to her.

When I returned home that evening, my husband accused me of sitting on a man's lap at the park.

I thought he was joking at first, then addressed his accusation. "You know that's not me. That would be out of my character."

He grew angry, calling me a cheater and a liar.

I called a friend girl over and began to cry in her arms. "I've done nothing."

"He's just looking for an excuse," she said calmly.

Greg came in and saw my friend consoling me, and told me he didn't want any trouble makers in his house.

I went directly into my closet and asked God for the first time if I could leave the marriage.

His words came back, "Stand still and see my salvation."

Soon afterward, Greg confessed his false accusation.

When the unclean spirit is gone out of a man,
he walketh through dry places, seeking rest;
and finding none, he saith, I will return unto my
house whence I came out.
And when he cometh, he findeth it swept and
garnished. Then goeth he and
taketh to him seven other spirits more wicked
than himself; and they enter in, and
dwell there: and the last state of that man
is worse than the first.
(Luke 11:24-26)

Chapter Five

WHEN THE ENEMY ENTERS IN

In any battle, the enemy's job is to throw darts in our path. His purpose is to deter, hurt and overtake us. When he enters into a home, his intent is to leave no survivors. He aims to utterly destroy our self-image and any possible trace of life.

Though Greg did his own thing, he always commented flirtatiously with me. He kept in shape and often asked me if he was getting buff.

"I don't know," was my latest reply.

When I asked him for advice on a dress I wanted to wear to my class reunion, he meanly called me a whore: "All you want is attention."

This comment really revealed to me the nature of the enemy.

To that, I answered confidently, "People will give me attention with a jogging suit on."

"Well, it doesn't look like you've been working out," he spited, knowing I made a commitment to exercise long before. And I was determined to keep that commitment no matter what the condition of my marriage was.

I asked God what was the root problem of my husband's behavior.

He said, "The root cause is molestation. Do you remember when Greg told you he had sex when he was six? He was boasting about it, but it wasn't sex. It was molestation. When he went back to the streets and started to mess around, it entered in full force. That's the reason he says he loves no one and likes to dog women out. He's doing that because the grown woman transferred her spirit on to him."

After God told me this, I tried to talk with Greg. He said he was too busy, but I still told him the root cause of his behavior, and asked him if he wanted to be delivered.

He replied sarcastically, "Deliver yourself. Don't say nothing else to me. Shut up. God doesn't tell you nothing. I don't want to hear it. I'll tell you what--I'm going to get your clothes and put you out!"

I stated boldly, "If you touch my stuff this time, God said he will strike you down. Now, go get my clothes if you're bad. I double dog dare you to get them. Get them!"

He stood beside my bedroom door, then walked out of the house. I messaged him later and apologized for over-stepping my boundaries.

God told me, "You must learn to distinguish between Greg and the spirits that are ruling him, or you are not going to make it out."

From that moment forward, I kept my distance, read my Word, and prayed all the more fervently; during which time one of the elders came over to anoint my home and ministered, pleading the Blood of Jesus Christ.

I asked God to hold my mouth, because I learned not everything He reveals is meant to be shared.

Me and my girls suffered violent Satanic attacks.

Christine and I were in our bedrooms. Greg went into her room where they began to argue. I heard anger in his voice.

"I hate you."

When he said that, I stopped in my tracks.

Then, he walked into the room where I was.

"You hate our daughter?"

"I hate you too," he stated bluntly.

As I stood there, the voice of the Lord said, "There is no failure in God."

The next day, Christine texted back and forth with Greg as we rode along in the van. When we made it home, her father walked into her room and they argued again. He choked her from her room to the front door, and put her out of the house.

She called the police and told them what happened. This was hardly the first, nor the last visit of the police to our house.

They asked me what I wanted them to do.

"He is my husband, and she is my daughter. Who do I say is right and who do I say is wrong?" I answered.

It was wrong for Greg to put his hands on Christine, but it was wrong for her to disrespect her father.

That day, Christine left home with her friend, and did not come back. She was sixteen. She told her sister that she never saw that look in their father's face before. "Even his voice didn't sound the same. That was not my daddy!"

It was true. The perfect husband, father, and minister had become a person unfamiliar to us all, and my heart had taken a step back with each incident.

Days later, Necie fell ill. She had chest pains, so we visited the hospital twice. Both times, she attempted to dispel our fears by saying nothing was wrong. The third time she texted me a letter that implied "goodbye." I immediately went to her.

"Momma, I can't get up."

Her friend and I lifted her up and drove her back to the hospital. The doctors told us not to let her leave until they figured out what was going on. Then, they carried my daughter downstairs for an ultrasound and found fluid around her heart. A specialist was called in and he instructed a close watch overnight until the following morning.

Necie called her father asking for a strawberry milkshake. He told that her she did not need it, nor did he bother to show up.

The next day I went to change clothes at home, then returned to the scene of doctors running in and out of the room. The heart specialist informed me that my daughter's heart was failing.

I called my sister screaming, "Her heart-- her heart. It's failing!"

Greg and many family members met us at the hospital that day during her emergency surgery.

The doctors held her two weeks to drain the fluid from around her heart and oversee her recovery.

I only saw Greg once during this time, but remained by my daughter's side all day and night. Family and close friends left money for me to eat and go home to change.

I thanked God when she came out of the surgery alright.

Within weeks, I also lay in bed recovering. A hysterectomy resulting from ovarian cysts formed during our earlier years of marriage, while trying to conceive. The issue had now developed into cancer.

To add to the travesty that year, my job cut back work hours which often left me short with the expenses.

My cousin called Greg to ask if he could help out with the bills.

"No," had become my husband's typical response to anything pertaining to our immediate family.

> *The thief cometh not, but for*
> *to steal, kill and to destroy.*
> *I have come that ye may have life and*
> *that ye may have it more abundantly.*
> (John 10:10)

Chapter Six

BATTLE TIME

Often times, we ask God to prepare our hearts for what we do not know. Truth revealed can either be an opportunity to awaken the warrior deep within, or a devastation to one's mental and emotional state.

When I prayed to God asking Him to show Gregory to me, in time He unfolded the situation piece by piece.

Though the facts were hard to accept, I managed to withhold. The enemy was now having his way in my husband. It was no longer Greg who spoke, but the enemy who lived in him. He was interacting with many Jezebel spirits now, and became totally out of control.

Greg had asked me to leave, and I said no. So, he called to taunt me, saying since I was being so tough by not leaving, he was turning the heat up even more.

"Out of the five women I am dating, three are asking me to come and live with them," he stated.

I saw that he was trying to do everything he could to destroy me.

My niece lives deep in the country. She called me and said, "Auntie, he has been out here for years with a woman."

"What woman?" I asked.

"She's a young girl and her last name is Smith. I see him spending nights, and she drives your car."

The same night when Gregory returned, I grabbed his phone when he went to sleep. Making a quick trip to Walmart, I searched through it.

All his iniquity was exposed. Phone numbers and pictures in his photo gallery from several women were listed. Some of the pictures were explicit and one young woman was pregnant.

Greg soon realized the phone was missing and was enraged. He messaged my phone from online. "Did you find what you were looking for?" He threatened to kill me once I made it home. Before leaving the store, I copied both messages and pictures. Frightened to return home because of his threat, I stayed away at my friend's.

The next morning, one woman he was involved with called his phone. I answered, "I'm Tina, Greg's wife."

"I'm the woman who's putting Greg on child support!"

I assured her she didn't have to do that, because my husband had been a good provider for his children.

After that call, I went home with his phone. When I arrived, he had a brick in his hand ready to cause damage.

"Didn't I tell you I was going to kill you?" His violent tone pierced me.

"If you move this car you're dead!"

Nervously contemplating if I should dare a speedy takeoff or stay put, and knowing trouble was either way, I went for the accelerator. He threw the brick.

Staying away from the house awhile longer to give him all the time he needed to cool off, also allowed me moments to face my own deep wounds. I cried about the woman's claim of an expected child by Gregory.

Despite what had or could happen, I believed I had to return home. When I did, Greg asked me to leave again, declaring the place was his. Yet, I felt I had the right to be there. So, I I moved out temporarily to gather strength for warfare, then returned.

I sat in my room one day when Greg stopped at the doorway.

"I was at the club, but I could not rest thinking on how I'm going to kill you. You don't know what you did when you took my phone. I'm all devil now! You unleashed a spirit that you have no idea what you have done."

As he brutally described how he was going to perform the act, how he would call my kids so they could hear me pleading for my life, he quoted a scripture.

63

I said, "Greg, you can't quote God's word while talking about killing me. Is it that serious?" I told him that it was his lusts he was dealing with, not me.

"I made two mistakes," he shot back. "One was marrying you, and the second was letting you move back in."

"Tell God it's a mistake," I challenged the thought. "I didn't want to marry you, so I know God joined us together."

Another particular day I heard God say, "It is in your house in a strange place."

Church members began to inform me about familiar spirits. One of them was my pastor's wife. As we conversed, I privately shared with her a few of my experiences.

She quickly interrupted, "I need you to talk with a prophet friend of mine in Kansas," then she merged a call between the 3 of us.

We each formerly greeted, then he began to confirm facts to me. "Your husband is stepping out in multiple affairs. One woman he is involved with deals heavily in witchcraft, and even candles. Her spirit is nasty, lustful and greedy for money. Every time he goes out there to mess around, he allows more spirits to enter into him."

The brother then exhorted me to keep praying, and said he would continue to pray for me. "...Because one can chase a thousand, two can chase ten thousand, and it will get worse before it gets better."

The same week, I visited a new church. When service was over a woman walked up to me. "Your husband is fixed." I was puzzled.

"Do you know me or my husband?"

"No, but hear the word of the Lord. The woman your husband is with is deep into witchcraft. She is putting things into his drink and under his tongue when they kiss."

Maybe a month later, I was riding in my car and God said, "Go to the park, there is someone I need you to see."

So, I did. And as I parked beside a car, a woman was approaching. I climbed out and cordially spoke to her.

"Hi," she responded.

"You're done for the day?" I asked further.

"Yes, I have church tonight."

We began to lightly converse about ministry, then she began to address my personal situation.

"This lady your husband is with, there is nothing good about her." She also encouraged me to stay prayed up, and watch God move in my life. Then she prayed for me, and I went home.

Weeks later, I was drying clothes. The machine kept shutting off. Looking around inside, I found a stone shaped like a heart.

God said, "That's it."

I discovered that the trinket was typically identified with witches and magical practices.

I took a picture of it, because I just knew no one would believe me.

I tried to tell Greg, but he refused to believe that the object was found in our house.

God spoke and said, "Don't tell him anything else, I will start revealing things to him.

Meanwhile, as Greg continued to come and go as he pleased, I had dreams about him standing over a baby in a crib.

While describing the events of the dream with him in it, and revealing that he a had baby on the way, he denied it. "Girl, don't come here with that foolishness."

"You know God deals with me in dreams," I persisted. I was learning God is faithful when it comes to revealing things.

After I confronted Greg about the woman on the phone whose name was Brenda, fiery blows escalated from both of them.

Not even the ordeals of Stephanie could have prepared me for what was to happen with Brenda, because this new female came in boldest.

The things he and Brenda did took a toll on my mind. They not only dated and wrecked each other's homes, they grew immensely wicked.

So, I left again temporarily to regroup.

During this period, Greg maliciously lied to me every day. He offered to inform me without my inquiry, "Brenda doesn't live here."

So, I would get up for work early, drive by our house, and take a picture of her car. Then I'd send them to him to prove he was lying.

One day, I needed to go there to check the mailbox, so I waited on the mailman.

Brenda boldly drove up with their baby and got out of her car, thinking she was going to walk in front of me on into my house.

I stopped her in her tracks, baby and all.

"You are not going into my house while I'm sitting on this porch."

"How long will you be here?" She sharply inquired.

"Until I'm good and tired, so go find somewhere else to hang until I leave."

She had the nerve to call the police. So, I sat there and waited until they came, knowing I was in the right.

"What is the problem?" The officer asked.

I answered, "Ask her, she called."

Brenda got out of her car and told the officer, "I live here, and she is always coming over!"

"Who are you?" The officer addressed me.

"I'm the wife."

"Is this marriage property?" He further inquired of me.

"Yes," I answered.

He looked at Brenda and said, "Get what

you need and get out of this lady's house! By law, this is still her house."

"Well, I need to feed Greg's baby," Brenda declared.

"He has a baby too? The judge is going to have a field day with him." The officer responded.

He and I started laughing, and the officer restated, "Get what you and the baby needs and get out of this woman's house."

Brenda walked in with the officer, gathered some items, and went her way. I stayed there a little longer for the mailman, collected my package and left.

Another day, my husband called to inform me that his car was in the shop, and that a friend would be picking him up for work the following day.

To that, I answered, "fine," although it sounded suspicious. *Why would you unnecessarily ask someone from across town to pick you up, and take you back across town for work?*

So, I woke up at 5 a.m. to drive by the house. When I arrived, Brenda's car was in the yard, as I had suspected.

When I stepped out to touch it, it was cold. Now, I knew that she spent the night in my house. I parked down the street, and waiting for them to come out.

Eventually, her car lights blinked.

O.K. here we go, you're going to handle this decently and in order. I bump rushed into her car and blocked them in.

Then, I approached Greg about her being in my house. As we argued, Brenda came out of the house and into their car.

"Oh, is that what married people do? Is that how y'all act?" She mocked.

We both looked at her, and I glanced over at him, shaking my head. Brenda began to take pictures of me, then she closed the door and cussed like a sailor.

"I have identified what is going on with her, and I will explain it to your later," I told my husband.

Then she asked Greg to call the police on me, because I was blocking her from going to work. Greg readily consented and called the police.

"Call them, you are at my house, you witch. Yes I know who you are, and I'm not backing down. My husband can sit here and look stupid like he doesn't know; but I do, you work of Jezebel!"

Brenda got so mad that she maneuvered their car around mine, until she found a way out.

I looked up and Greg was at the door of my car about to get in for me to take him to work; but he decidedly shut my car door and ran back to Brenda's car. Then, they took off for work.

I experienced back to back episodes of Brenda texting and running up on me.

First, she called me. "Your husband is here with me. I would let you hear him snoring, but it will hurt you."

Whenever Greg and I argued, she immediately sent me photos of myself beside a monkey, texting, "You're acting like one." Then, she sent me pictures of myself beside an old woman.

Whenever she saw me in a store, she waited until I came out, then drove up to me, laughed and pulled off.

I never spoke a word to her in my defense.

After calling Greg to tell him, but seeing he refused to accept her evil acts, I learned to just pray all the more.

Greg eventually asked me if I wanted to

come home, and I answered yes. I do not know exactly what happened, but it was all arranged with Brenda.

He also confessed that the reason he had wanted me to leave was because he did not want me to find out about the baby.

"I already knew, I just wanted to hear it from you," I said.

He further divulged that he had wanted Brenda to have an abortion.

Offering me his comfort and bed to sleep in, I knew Greg was up to no good and wanted more. A day later, by phone at work he shared with me how he felt.

It was hard since we were living like roommates, he explained. "I don't like it. Some changes are going to be made. Any woman in my house, I make love to."

With my guards up I retorted, "No, not me! I'm not here for that. You're in and out of the house. You don't need me. How much sex do you want?"

One evening Brenda called me about their child. "I had his child, why didn't you have him one?" She knew the reason.

I dismissed Miss Smith's phone call, but

felt completely undone! I hung up the line, thinking I couldn't handle anymore. Things were happening back to back.

I immediately called my friend and confided in her. She urged me to stand, in spite of.

I listened in despair to every word my friend said, then replied, "No longer can or will I deal with the enemy. I'm no match for him. Greg is going from one woman to the next. I am giving up." Suddenly, I shifted into a state of total emotional numbness. Everything that was happening felt meaningless.

Linda repeatedly called my name over the phone, but I could not speak. Then, I cried uncontrollably and hung up.

I went to the kitchen to grab a glass of water and sat on my bedroom floor to make a second suicide attempt. As I put the pills to my mouth, my friend walked in and slapped them out of my hand. I don't know how she made it over so quickly, or how she was able to get inside, because the doors were usually locked, but she did. Thank God! She spoke the Word to me, but to no avail. I was not only broken, I was crushed!

So, she hugged and rocked me like a baby as I began to cry out to God, seeking Him for guidance.

Not understanding the meaning of the word "depression" before, I have now come to my own definition: One who is sent to an unreachable place.

At that time, all I saw was a darkness I would never wish upon anyone.

When I woke up in the morning, my mind was so cloudy I could barely think. I stayed in bed weekends at a time; just lying there, and only coming out of my room when no one was home.

Pulling away from my family and friend, I found I had lost interest in everything going on around me for many days.

Starvation wrapped around me: I no longer had an appetite.

This was a very bad state to be in. One day I heard God say, "Either you live through this, or you die through this."

I answered, "God, I want to live." So, I got up, put on clothes, and went out for the first time in months.

Although God raised me up from that

that dead place, I still had to walk through a process of food deprivation. I had to put something in my mouth to survive.

One day I told myself, "You've got to eat to live."

I was starving myself to death; but, Lord behold! Thank God for salvation.

One night, God spoke to me in a dream.

You are strong enough. Get worship music, and I want you lying before me praying. You are going into warfare. Whatever he does, do not say a word. The next day, I fell into a trance and He spoke to me again so beautifully. He covered me with the armor of God from head to toe.

I increased in keenness and began picking up Greg's movements in the spirit. He is sly and swift. This is why he cannot be still, is moving around all night, and is not sleeping.

"I know I do wrong, but have asked God to forgive me," Greg confessed one morning .

"That does not agree with my spirit," I responded.

That Sunday church service did not start until three o'clock, so I read the Word and spent time in meditation and prayer, talking to God about what Greg stated to me. "You mean to tell me that he can do his wife and family any kind of way, day after day, and all he has to do is ask for forgiveness only to do it again?"

As I read, I found that forgiveness is not only asking God for forgiving one's sins, but thanking Him.

Why would one ask God for forgiveness when he has already been forgiven?

As I further studied the topic, I learned that a person is supposed to ask forgiveness from someone they have hurt.

One confesses, asks for forgiveness and then repents, all with a sincere heart. After that, God will accept repentance and start to renew that individual's soul.

I prayed to God, asking Him to please humble Greg, knowing it would take His saving power to deliver and deal with my husband's heart so he could own up to all the damage he had caused.

When we pray God's will into our lives, we have to step out of the way. If His will consists of us being broken or isolated for a season, we have to cope with that. If God allows it, cope with it.

However, He promised to give us an expected end.

What do we do when struggle and pain still remains, even when we feel like we've done everything right? We endure.

At this point, I had asked myself why I was still there, but, I remembered. When I left before, I heard the devil say, "The day you leave him for good, I am going to have a field day."

Greg planned a dinner one evening.

"When were you going to tell me that more family was coming?" I chided with Greg for rarely running anything by me. This time it was to be the next day, on Thanksgiving.

"She's family too; you should not have a problem with her being here."

It wasn't that I had a problem with his baby. The child was welcome. The visit was unexpected and preparations would have to be made for her as well as others attending.

Greg lashed out with name calling and accused me of sleeping with his friend. He further offered to take me to the truck stop, claiming he was a pimp. The dreadful conversation maneuvered its way into the following day, when he informed me that divorce papers were in process.

The topic of divorce crept up more often with each conversation. It was New Year's and we discussed how we should fix up the house, what I wanted, and how I wanted it done.

He then shifted, "Why would I fix up the house? I'm divorcing you."

"You know what," I replied, "stop saying it and holding the divorce over my head. Call your attorney to see what you need to do to get the divorce finalized. No one wants a divorce. Why take a chance losing all that we have?"

"I told you," he declared, "because you cheated on me, I didn't want you anymore."

I ended the conversation with, "You know I never cheated on you. Whether God allows the divorce or not, I'm content with whatever he's doing in my life."

It wasn't long before Greg told me he was going on a cruise in August.

You're going to sit here in my face and tell me that you and another woman are going on a cruise together next summer?"

"Oh, no!" He explained, "I'm going by

myself."

"Who goes on a cruise by themselves?"

"It won't be with Brenda. Oh, and by the way, we are getting a divorce."

I stated angrily, "I watched you walk out of my house two years ago and take another woman out of town. Greg, you should never do for a woman in the streets what you haven't done for your own wife. You never did take me anywhere. So, you are right, we need to be divorced; because I'm not watching you walk out this house again to take another woman on a trip."

Later that day, I went to the movies with a very sick friend. Greg text messaged me, "Enjoy the movies with your man."

Again, he called the next day, "The only thing holding up the divorce is you. You're trying to get money out of me that I'm simply not going to give.

All the women I talked to say you're a fool. They said when they left, they left everything. You're going to stay there and let me treat you like that, for what? I am not giving you a penny."

When is this going to end, God? I am tired and over the divorce now.

Knowing how good Greg once was to me is what made it so hard to let go, but it hurt too much to keep him.

I grew to realize that just because he stopped loving me didn't mean I stopped loving him.

I couldn't understand why my love was so deep for him, so I went to God and asked.

"You're not loving him with your love, you are loving him with my love. It is because I love him so," he answered.

My mother-in-law died. She had called for Greg to come to the hospital, but he was at work. His sister tried to notify him that his mother wished to see him.

He said okay, but did not go there that evening. He called after work and asked how his mother was doing. They told him she was asleep, but had asked for him all day; awaking, asking for him, and then falling back asleep.

Greg never went that night. The next day she was gone. No one knows why she wanted to speak to her son so badly. As saved as my mother-in-law was, I can guess why she wanted to talk with him.

I had a dream about Mama Dupree.

She sat on the front of the church row. Only the two of us were there and she spoke awhile. "Daughter, I've been talking with my Lord." I smiled. "I know you have, Ma." She continued, "God told me to tell you vengeance is His."

Again, I went to the church and Mama was singing. She said, "Daughter, I tried to tell you..." She stopped.

I woke up crying from missing her so much.

"God, you're even remembering me in a dream!" I said.

One Friday, I was unusually tired at work, but pressed on; never being so anxious to leave to talk to God about what was wrong. He spoke to me that death was going to hit the family again. I wanted to take off the following day, because I was not at peace.

Usually, Greg called me at 3 or 4 a.m. when he was out; so, I waited in panic mode. The phone rang at 3 a.m. My first thought was, *Oh, no--Greg! If it's him, Lord, please help me to handle it.*

"Greg--Greg, are you okay?"

He said he was at the hospital with his brother Darren, who had been stabbed. I was in a state of shock.

Greg came home later. As soon as he turned into bed, he received a call that Darren had passed away. He left the house to tell his other siblings of the tragedy. I went to my deceased brother-in-law's house to comfort his wife.

The day prior to Darren's wake, Greg called me to say he was officiating the service. Brenda was coming to the funeral.

"Oh, my God, no. No, Greg."

He overrode, "I don't care what you say or how you act, she is coming."

I told him that it was so disrespectful and this was something I would not put up with. his wife, mistress, and girlfriend would all be at the funeral. I would not be a part of that. So, I refused to go.

However, I went to the wake and repass to be with all our family. Greg and Brenda paraded around unashamedly on the church premises. He and I exchanged cordial words about our cell phones.

I noticed people looking at the situation which was so awkward. Family members commented to me how disrespectful the couple was.

I spoke with Greg's cousin at the wake

who was going through a similar situation with her husband.

"How did you walk away?"

She answered that she was tired of the abuse. "So, one day I just drove eight hours and landed at a new residence. I went in as a battered spouse and they helped me on my feet."

Talking with her, and seeing how happy and relieved she was. I exclaimed, "God, that is how I want to be--free!"

Greg came home after the wake irritated I told him I knew it was a bad idea.

He said he didn't want to hear anything I had to say.

At times, I saw Greg watching me, and I could see the hate in his eyes when he didn't know I was looking.

I asked God, "Why can't I have a conversation with him?"

He replied, "You are talking with the enemy, and there is no reasoning with the enemy. Make your words short and sweet."

I answered, "Okay, just continue helping me, because I don't know just what to do. I have received so much evil when I have shown so much love."

God answered, "You are demonstrating the love I have for you. I am love and kindness, and I am in you. So, you have no other choice but to show my good nature."

That night, Greg and I parted for the very last time. He moved in with Brenda and I stayed in our home until he filed for divorce.

I no longer dwelled on how good a wife I was, how good I once had it, or how one day, Greg is going to get what he has coming to him.

Instead, I learned how to rely on God; to hear but not hear, and to see but not see.

I started running to God with my problems first, before my pastors, family and friends.

Yet, without the people God used to intervene during this time, I would not have made it out alive

He will keep him in perfect peace
whose mind is stayed on Him.
(Isaiah 26:3)

Chapter Seven

GOD'S SPOKEN WORD

Greg left a voice mail on my phone saying
our court date was set for August. When I
heard it, I stopped breathing. *God, what will I
do? I don't make enough money to survive on my
own.*

Then, I remembered my prayers asking
God to have His own way. Immediately after
a short praise, I received a call saying that I
had an interview scheduled for a job I

wanted. Then, another company responded to an application from over a year before.

"Go on, God! No one can do it like you can. Thank you," I said.

At Walmart, the other day I saw our old friend Roman again. He commented, "I applaud you for staying with your husband. I know it was hard, but you set an example of how Christian women should be when their marriages are in trouble."

"Only God had me standing. Tina would have walked out a long time ago."

"Keep standing in your faith, it is ministers to me."

"I have no other choice. God didn't tell me to leave."

"I wish my wife would have stayed, but she divorced me."

I spoke to God about how it had to have taken a strong woman to go through this, but He answered, "No, it took a Godly woman to go through this. "

Another woman who knew me asked how I handled what I was going through. I said, "Nobody but God handled my battle. He held me and hid me in his secret place."

"I couldn't handle it for one day and you

went through it for years."

"You may never know how much you're able to handle until you find yourself in a situation," I encouraged.

So, the road to sharing this season of victory in my life began with family and friends, then continued to grow into an invitation to a women's fellowship group, and on to my first conference.

Today, I continue to serve by imparting both the experience and knowledge I have gained to help bring healing to shattered women wherever I go.

Whether it is on the job or on the road, I have collected countless thank-you letters by wives whose marriages have been saved; and women whose minds were rescued from committing suicide, just by hearing my story and testimony.

I had no idea a ministry of hope and encouragement would come out such degrees of pain and suffering.

If I knew of His plan, would I have agreed to it? Often, my heart has pondered. When I think of how His love steps into our hearts, when man walks out, there is no question. The sweetest love on earth could never compare with His.

I do not clearly know how the enemy entered into my marriage so fiercely, nor why it came to such a tumultuous end.

I contribute my own youthful lust and lack of discretion to be partly to blame for why I had to suffer so much.

I was not the fearful or intimidated type as a youngster, so it did not occur to me to wisely question Gregory for his troubled past before we married.

One reason for allowing myself to become so mesmerized with Gregory may have been because of the lack of adolescent affection.

Yet, I believe God spoke to me when we first met and told me that Greg was my husband.

The bad choices Greg made may have been because he was too proud to confess there was a molestation issue.

It could have simply been in his initial decision to have an affair.

It could have been through the pills he began to take.

I did dress him sharper than his ability to handle; and gaining "too much, too soon" is also a point on which I have pondered, many times.

Maybe it was because he once made an agreement with God in prison, but turned his back on it.

Many evil spirits which came to attack the mind after his heart has been made clean, may also explain the stronghold.

There was apparent iniquity passed down from generational fathers of which we warred against.

It is possible that all of these factors among the two of us contributed to Satan's scheme.

Whatever the cause, the love of Jesus Christ never fails, so, I continue to pray for him as for my own self and children.

Who being the brightness of His glory
and the express image of His person,
when He had by himself purged our sins,
sat down at the right hand
of the Majesty on high.
(Hebrews 1:3)

EPILOGUE

Each morning I jog a mile in the park before going to work, passing slopes of oak trees and breathing in the cool, fresh air.

It is my routine in a brand new day of discovery. A season of which is both exciting and frightening.

I feel like a spring chicken just entering into the world, enjoying the movies and eating dinner by myself. On occasion, I join my female friends in delightful fellowship. We talk and laugh for hours.

I am paving a different path this time. It is another way of thinking. *Feeling lonely does not mean I am alone, because the Holy Spirit com-*

forts me when I am by myself, sick or afraid.

I am learning not to look for a man to fill the void of my heart these days, because the emptiness of my soul is less present. My dreams of marriage lay still for God's revealing, but for now I am good.

I cannot know all the marvelous plans He has in store, but the future awaits and is filled with hope and opportunities

What I do know is that I am The King's child. I am royalty. And I am worth more than gold to my Eternal Father who loves me.

And I know that Satan comes to steal beauty, heaping it up in ashes to make flourishing places desolate. But my Lord gathers up the ash into His palm, and with reforming life He fashions beauty upon mountains of peace.

> *To appoint unto them that mourn in Zion,*
> *to give unto them beauty for ashes,*
> *the oil of joy for mourning, the garment*
> *of praise for the spirit of heaviness…*
> (Isaiah 61:3)

NOTES...

NOTES...

NOTES...

www.ingramcontent.com/pod-product-compliance
Lightning Source LLC
Chambersburg PA
CBHW060344050426
42449CB00011B/2819